ORDERS *of* SERVICE

WILLIE LEE KINARD III

ORDERS *of* SERVICE

Alice James Books
NEW GLOUCESTER, MAINE
alicejamesbooks.org

CELEBRATING 50 YEARS OF ALICE JAMES BOOKS

Printed in the United States

10 9 8 7 6 5 4 3 2 1

Alice James Books are published by Alice James Poetry Cooperative, Inc.

Alice James Books
Auburn Hall
60 Pineland Drive, Suite 206
New Gloucester, ME 04260
www.alicejamesbooks.org

Library of Congress Cataloging-in-Publication Data

Names: Kinard, Willie Lee, III, author.
Title: Orders of service / Willie Lee Kinard III.
Description: New Gloucester, Maine : Alice James Books, 2023.
Identifiers: LCCN 2023026667 (print) | LCCN 2023026668 (ebook) | ISBN 9781949944570 (trade paperback) | ISBN 9781949944303 (epub)
Subjects: LCGFT: Poetry.
Classification: LCC PS3611.I563 O73 2023 (print) | LCC PS3611.I563 (ebook) | DDC 811/.6--dc23/eng/20230616
LC record available at https://lccn.loc.gov/2023026667
LC ebook record available at https://lccn.loc.gov/2023026668

Alice James Books gratefully acknowledges support from individual donors, private foundations, the National Endowment for the Arts, and the Amazon Literary Partnership.

Cover Image: Artwork created by Vintagemozart 2022. Interior illustration: Shutterstock/Theus.

Epyllia

III

IV

for my family
& the work we do.

I will pray with the spirit, and I will pray with the understanding also:

—I CORINTHIANS 14:15 KJV

It matters what you call a thing:

—SOLMAZ SHARIF

For the mouth speaks what the heart is full of.

—MATTHEW 12:34 NIV

Self-Portrait as the Cricket

0.0 mi

The way my legs sit, slightly curved around the knees,
old women squint their eyes yet still ask me if I'm single.

The summer night bows to the flutter of my lashes
& I know this is only about my walk.

I suppose they are for music-making, I tell them,
leveraging only the floor for balance.

There is nothing to brag about, it is true:
I have drawn thunder out of a woman.

I have never broken a heart on purpose
& not felt the shatter of it in my hips.

My hips often announce my presence before I do.
I have made my bed in a thicket of grass blades.

A boy plucked a chirp from me like I was a grass blade.
My own name is a field of chirping.

My own name is a church of fields.
I listen for it when I put a man on his back.

A man on his back is a call & response.
My own name is a choir of churches.

My own name is a chorus of strumming.
Some nights, the only refrain I care sung.

I

The Choir, or Chatteracks

Hexapod pumps line branches of the choir stand as we brace ourselves for
weak spots three-by-five strong. Fanning its barks with tambourine shells & what
-ever else from the funeral home, I rock on the edge of old wood.
Beads of sweat loosen both limbs & the elastic of already falling
garters. Like sheets, drawers, & almost anything unholy: we grunt,
& stomp, & I know damn well, we shake some shit up. We fell a veil rooted
in work outdating us. Precede gods with our own flagrant divinities,
the dew of White Diamond & Sean John dung beetle musking as magnolia.

For eons, I katydid & Mary-don't-you-whip the Methuselah
from the knees of my ensemble & every pew-bound bee asking how
we making more noise than them—as they said, molding the Lord's honey & making
them look bad. In a word, yes: shaking does the body good. But, I will say
how I felt it: the dry rot of not-dusk & corners of Pastor's big lips
already annoyed that we even dare to be hollering for Bug-Jesus
like this anyway: like she ain't already up & gave Bug Jesus her best
crook-legged praise. Like she don't need no help. Like it don't take all that.

Like we outchea doing some shit she ain't ask us in the first place. (Like, we
tryna get our holy on!) So, like the rattling deviants we are, we dig
& fill each mouth with surprise & invert our fears into something able
to leave anyone shook. We husk. We hum. We don't hear what they call us:
Noisemakers. Latecomers. Backsliders. Pillowbiters. Bulldaggers. Nightcrawlers:
O hooligans! O heretics! O word-warpers! O whip-poor-wills! O mourn
-ing doves!: We sunshine singers. We dewdrop deities. We muses, boo.
We chatteracks. We lightning bugs. We country, nigga: We ain't studdin' 'bout them.

Boomerang, or a Chorus of Onlooking Fireflies Captions the Previous Poem

They smelled humid & lightning followed.

____ smelled _____ & lightning followed.

What We Wayward Do

All spells begin with water.
Rod in hand, flick of it against the stinging sky,
Mama nem stir the air to tears.

Casting is what they call the girls putting in work
'round here & yes, we witches are fishermen,
whip glamours in men's overalls
so long as fish rise to the surface
mere hours before morning's stilettos.

Believe me—at the edge, we make them levitate,
each saddling our silence as if any noise unweighted
would loose a daemon slick-scaled & wide-eyed
with no bellies by which to bind it.

Where I'm from, folk learn conjure early,
the kind of favor you pray over a pole for
& what is Greek is still a gospel:

Here, Jesus is a sigil with light bread
& there is always a Pilate & a piercing before cooking,
a struggle so steady, we laugh at our buckets,
that is, yes, we flay the fish with care.

Cricket-fed & fried light, worked to the bone,
this how we kill our familiars:
there is nothing, then something.
Something, then nothing. It is wristwork.
It is sobering. It is holy. We gather.
We murmur. We swallow in worship.

A Tangle of Gorgons

The lesbians that lived in the apartment to the left
of my grandmother's were always described in whispers.

Caught in her teeth, her jokes: a pile of serpents
thrown at her neighbors for stealing her appetite

—always hurried, always hushed, hissing her "sissies"
& "scissoring" as if the slurs would set them straight.

It's a complex: to return callous to the same snake
den reminding you of your own head's sibilance.

I am of that ilk, I suppose: dreadful
by happenstance, mere blinking having stopped

many a man in his tracks before me. Forbidden
to enjoy it, this calcified lineage.

Like mighty Stheno & Sister Euryale, our family
name insists wartime: those of us battling this curse

of loving men never cease to stop making rocks
of them, I, hating their waters, never able to skip any.

They don't make it that far. Somehow, always sinking,
always cracking, always losing parts of themselves.

Before my father's cleaving to fracture, I eroded
his visage to ruin. I barely recognize

him anymore, call him by his first name;
in my head, shortening the suffix. The second

time I cried for a man, my heart became a stone
I'm not sure I can pass off for a body part.

I don't often mention it, but I need
to speak on our history of numbness

—the golems we bear to know what it is
to bury a heart because someone abused it;

how I've seen it: every sorrow a reflection
I've avoided combing through, favoring the gleam

of being shorn bald. I must be specific:
I have mirrored these monsters before, severed

a personhood & expected it inconsequential.
But snakes won't stop coming out of my face now.

Their headless balm of displaced oil, preferring
the word *serpentine* to *wolfish*, litters

the sink with onyx scales graying as old money,
losing count of hours lost losing count

of bottles of Nair, losing count of quarters
lost promising men that they won't bite.

Unless unsettled, my mother bites, insisting my series
of settling unsettles her. I am getting upset again,

steaming at how I am always seen
as the unintended coven member, learned

in the ways the women folded their prayers
as they did their napkins—tucked in the center

of a lap in the center of a man in the center of a table
in the center of a lap in the center of a house

in the center of a lapse in the center of a judgment
that asks: why I'm still sitting inside, my uncles ponder.

The weatherworn heir, moistened of caches of secrets
of stoners & sisters of sinners in secrets in service

of sexes insistent on serving their bullshit
—I'm sure they too would prefer me headless.

It is frightening: I come from a stony people,
my own uncle's middle name meaning *gem*.

My grandma was cunning like that, slipped regal
wishes into her children as if to imbue

them with crowns instead of petrifying them.
We are skilled in this type of sorcery,

tangling regret with dissatisfaction
when sulking a *sorry* might not be enough.

But, it slinks off our lips anyway,
disdain's silhouette appearing only in light

of our gorgonry, this, our mother tongue,
how we stilled our anguish, scarred our statues

of psyches so, our countenances bled millennia
before we ever turned to stone.

Hear them whisper what my secret is:
I have hardened for men many a day,

wantoned my waist round unwanted Perseans
just to see if I could still do it again.

I wound. They whined. They slunk. They swung.
They spat. They struck. They slung that weak shit

like they just knew they were hitting it right
—their ego, its scissor, a sword-swallowing cut

intent on making a trophy of me—I'm stunned.
My God. They never remember the head.

Barbicide

0.1 mi

do not hold eye contact too long. mention
            the weather, your grandmother's quilting, the length
of time it takes to stitch a bass clef into
            the voice of your conscience. admire the *JET* beauty
of the week. do not hold your back like her.
            take the flatwing. do not suck the lemon pepper
from your fingers. do not hold eye contact
            too long. hold your knee out. debate whether
it is gall or lust curdling in your throat. bottle it
            as witch hazel. wonder if the mirror is as sharp
as he appears. do not hold eye contact too long.
            reach for him. lick the blood from your hand.
swallow. nod with an answer when finished.

Hymn: Throw Honey to the Wind & Watch Bees Come Back

33.3 mi

Short-shorts draw droves of you boys I don't like,
your flat brims & gold-plated stingers to where
the mirage of back bounces against my
gapped thighs, where I will convince
you most I am your flower.

But trust: I don't fold well, ain't never been dainty;
simply long & splintered, for legs spread ajar
have always made me feel uncomfortable
but I have made a habit of taking
what I don't quite want.

I throw honey to the wind & watch bees come back,
find gold leaf in folds of me where petals
I last stroke I ain't quite wash well;
I'm sorry, I stopped believing
in this type of lonely.

Don't ask me, darling, I would like to think
it does feel better with the hat on,
knowing I will not give you sugar
& won't call you Daddy; tonight,
that is not your name.

Catalog of My Obsessions or Things I Answer To

alphabetization; ancestry & lineage; alternate endings; anonymity; antonyms; arrangements; Babel; Balm in Gilead; Blackness & beauty; book lists; Book of Daniel; bumblebees; call & response; calling & messaging; cemeteries & necropolises; chimeras; choirs & choir culture; choral responses; church; church services; cicadas; citizen names; colloquialisms; composition & composure; conjunctions; conjure & magic; conversations; countriness & the pastoral; creation; crickets; darkness & light; death; definitions; descants & modulation; destruction; distance & distancing; divine, divine pantheons; doctrine; dogs & wolves; dreams; etymology; ex-lovers; familial curses & expectations; fire & warmth; fireflies; fish; flight; folklore & wives' tales; food; funerals; gardens; Greek myth & allusion; gorgons; gospel deep cuts; grief & mourning; grief as a site of love; grooming practices; herbs; Him; homegoings; homecomings; honey; hymns & psalms; hymnody & songwriting; Icarus; image-making; inheritance; instructions; intentionality; interruptions & returning; juxtaposition & polyptychs; lists & numbering; matrilineal power structures; memory; middle names; the Minotaur; mirrors & reflections; mixtapes; multiplicity & replication; muses; necrosis & the word *necropolitan*; night; Nike, or Victory; noise & silence; note-taking & observation; numbers of years; numbness & kinesis; the opposite of *because*; ordering of contents; orthodoxy; patterns & processes; performance; petitioning of a God; the phrase *pray until something happens*; pole beans; polyphony; portraiture; possession; pottery; prayer & manifestation; puzzles & mazes; rabbit holes & marginalia; rain, retelling; recovery; repetition; rest as praxis; routines & rituals; selected pieces; self-acceptance; self-declaration; sex & the erotic; shouting & whispers; singing & music; slow burns; social traditions & taboo; sonnet-like turns, speech & recitation; songs & choruses; spellings, sources & footnotes; spellwork & incantations; spiritual occupation; stars & constellations; stoning & petrification; submission; suffixes; sugar; superstition; surrealism; sweetness; things I answer to; titles & naming; traditions; transformation & shape-shifting; ventriloquy; vibrato; Virgoan poetics; vocal pedagogy; water; where I feel at home; witnessing; why's

To Be Feral

66.7 mi

In the dream where chimeras emerge from the sea,
Daniel fantasizes of water-winged options & I am the beast.

Our frames melt into a shifting torrent of limbs,
—first ten, then fewer, then ten again,
an ever-change reminding us we only exist as theory,
once here, briefly, then no longer.

In the second half, I trace his dripping, his drowning,
the time it takes to write a praying man wet
& emptied in the hollows of a thing he calls *monster*,
the work considered to sing yourself well afterward.

In the night, to be feral is to be a possibility.
He sleeps & unbound odds bite at both of us.
I try to beat them without losing any teeth.
He wakes up & one of mine has gotten looser.

Labyrinth

Understand: a name is a corn maze.
In it, a beast can be shackled. I will call my irons
Suffix. At my neck, a succession of fathers jangle
in the crook of my collar & cloven lineage,
my most immediate gnarled between
the hoof-trudged ground & my own horns.

This yoke ain't easy. I pull my father
behind me, slosh through stubborn puddles
of his absence, muddying halls at every corner
with innards of Taurean carcass. He is not dead,
just heavy. & I, only half bull. I will be frank:
it is exhaustive. Willie is usually diminutive.

According to Ma's records returning-to-sender
her not-husbands' light bills, there were 30 of us
in our city, a bushel's worth of walls running
the confines of this town, sprouting like a labyrinth.

In the legend of it, a father builds the thing
& each wall reads the same. It is exhaustive.
In another version, the top half breaks shorter,
my name slants toward 'star.' I leap to claim a legacy.

Bush River Blues

Sam Cooke & the Soul Stirrers, "Peace in the Valley"
40.5 mi

On
God,
I have
believed
in many men.
Not a fault, but
a waterwork—a Black boy
that loved a man; my brother,
one of the same. That kind of blue:
April; the chill of spring settling into
the crunch of our respective Faded Glory
denim & over-sounding windbreaker jackets;
no cap, spirited—a haint; color-of-sky-on-visitation
-mornings-type glass of a blue; my brother & I, out
the door, off the porch painted the same pollen-dusted
color. It is clear: our father doesn't see the magic
trick of our smiles vanish like plans agreed upon
months ago. Today isn't a trip to the movies
blue. It is a gifting of my Pokémon Sapphire
to my left-his-game-at-home—yes, hurt
—brother's indigo-tinted blue. Then,
not my favorite color. Or, the one prior,
but one to count on: an ain't-gotta-say
-what's-understood hue
sure to cut
deep
.
Don't
get me
wrong: it hurt

the first time, but
I've come to expect it
—men aren't socialized
for small commitments.
I get it: the kind of corner
store candy my brother
loves to wash the after
-math of its hotdogs
down; the kind
of man Ma hates
working her
nerves; the
kind
of
smile
I put
on to
not seem
disappointed
again. It's not
my fault: I'm doing
my best to look
out for us both,
like I am told,
feelings
bottling
to pressures
the color of forearm
veins, my clenched
fist dismissing
another trip
to Grandma's
house as well as
pools of glaucoma
lighting up when we see
her not ten minutes
later—a happy

kind of
blue.
A jay
-bird blue.
A corvid blue.
A mourning
blue: a dove,
blue.
A
silent
blue.
It's mighty
blue. // Shol' is,
blue. A red-mud
-on-jeans-when-it-rains
-type blue. Hope-it-won't
-be-long blue. &, so, it is:
the ping of syncopating
showers echoing my & my brother's
sniffles, bouncing as baby
bundles, the pauses for thunder
pregnant with soon-crying
little boys in the truck
back home. *It should*
be clear, I think,
the sky
of
our
faces,
the tears
that betray
us. We cannot
stand to hold them
longer, each a ghost
of a blue lingering,
our bodies
heaving

as
if
shed
-ding shards
of glass no longer
holding us together
—a broken bottle
blue. Hypnotic kind
of blue. A drunken
-hearted blue.
A cried-to-sleep
blue. A flaking
blue. Affirming
blue
.
A
grease
-on-shoulder
-of my-jacket
blue. Hard
-to-get
-out blue.
A magic
kind
of blue.
A shrug
-ging kind
of blue. A hug
-ging kind of blue.
A balmy kind of blue.
A bawling kind of blue.
A calling, a hook, a haunt
-ing kind of blue. A stir
-ring, a steering, a tier
-ing, a turning,
a burning,
stubborn

kind of stun
-ning blue?
—a run
-ning
blue,
eroding
blue—a rust
-ic blue;
a river,
eldest
of sorrows
made grave
—see: fallen
—blue.
A
damn
-ed blue.
A give-a-damn
-to-a-river-&-watch
-him-still-flow
-down-the-long
-excuse
-home
-before
-apologizing
-type blue; a hop
-scotch blue;
a skipped
stones
blue;
make sour
the words
I'm sorry
& jump
before
your
short

-comings
catch up to you
blue—a repeat; a river;
our father, the kind of water
reflecting every which way
but right; my brother & I,
the kind to still try
& forgive
him
.

The Sugar

I find the sweat of sugar awfully saddening,
how the tongue bursts into tears at the sight
of candied mandarins swimming in light syrup;

they say we shouldn't eat things out of cans anymore.
But, I'm spooning out my joy tonight.

I should be more explicit when talking about my body;
I have a habit of sugarcoating indulgences
when I can't apologize for what I enjoy
—the easy-peel boys at my neck & waist,
my penchant for rushing my healing.

My mother says this is how men can become necrotic,
canning our vices 'til the hurt catches up to us.
Or did she say *loose*?

I don't know if she means men or my father these days.
We all tend to end in disappointment or bad teeth,
nonetheless, hard grinning.

II

Boomerang, or a Chorus of Onlooking Fireflies Captions the Previous Poem

They smelled humid & lightning followed.

They hooded clouds & lightning followed.

____ hooded _____ & lightning followed.

____ smelled _____ & lightning followed.

B{u/i}tter Pecan Apocrypha

Directions: complete the passage by selecting the fitting pronoun.

Like the cruel misfortune of unwrapping
an already ruined package, {you/I} imagine
{your/my}self unsalvageable. Shards star-twinkling
in a slurry sky of nut butter, {you/I} want to wrap
{my/your}self in something already bothered
so {you/I} can go on about {my/your} business.
{You/I} already work for the Lord, {you/I}'ll claim that.
{You/I} do not want to be saved. {You/I} want to be born.
{You/I} want to be stomached, eaten in spite. {You/I} want to spite
in one sinner's unmentionable work. Like most nights,
{you/I} want to be worked all over and weep
with joy by morning. {You/I} want to morn
only once & dusk when it is then {your/my} time.
{You/I} want {your/my} time to matter. {You/I} want
{your/my} matter recognized. Of contributions
to scriptured fruit & nuts {your/my} folks know
too damn well, {you/I} want to be caught in the throat.
{You/I} want my shards to sting, to grate little misfortunes
unnoticeably swallowed. {You/I} want to blow open a cord.
{You/I} want to know a windpipe. {You/I} want to k{you/I}ss
a good wind. {You/I} want to be another round, lavishly savored
in the jaw of somebody's grandchild—slunk on the tongue
in dissent, crunching out of {you/my}th & plastic, roasted,
chilling. Listen—an elder stretches their arms to tell how much
they loved it, one younger cracking open what'll soon be familiar:
then, God blew {you/I}nto an icebox & called the tasteful *Sweet.*

The Vision

Pythokritos, Winged Victory of Samothrace,
early second century BC, Parian marble

Mariah Carey, "Fly Like A Bird"

Hitherto, at the very end of the matter, the boy I see
    relinquishes the hold of his steed   summons brimstone
    polishes his frenzy's ghosts   against the wishes of a timid
    man's worries, bounds two octaves
            for the glories of Crete   for the supper table invocation
            for the pot of greens only a savior could throw a ham
            hock into   for the empty bellies of all those crying
            for cries into the watchful dusk   for all the names he
            gives the night   for all night could refuse to call him—
                    call him *grimoire*   call him *trouble*   call him
                    weeping   call him *diva*, a new Nike—
                            call for freedom   call for fury   call for
                            furnace   call for three boys, no, four—
                                    he burns the loom   slashes stitches
                                    rips silk   frees feathers   inks the text—
                                            this sparrow seen   a nest
                                            of coins   a payment given
                                            a call collect   a pay phone,
                                            sir   a bird, almost   a busted
                                            joint   a wretched penance
                                            from whence he might just
                                                    flee   fly   spring
                                                    jump, darling,
                                                    jump—
                                                            & of the sun,
                                                            steals it.

Hymn: Chainsweat

2.1 mi

From the pantheon of hot niggas online tonight, out pops
its most glorious cicada. Who else, Reader, but Summer,
rattling louder than a muhfugga under the fuss of high air,
crushed velvet & Black Ice air fresheners, sweeping the block
in only the loudest Deuce n' a Quarter he could snatch?
I can smell him from here. This swamp, a ripe heat,
one crushed bud of lavender under my tongue,
one degree over peppermint & I am trying to impress.
I haven't wanted to be someone else's as much as I do now.
I didn't say belong: I'm talking about romance. Smell it
from here: the tease of his call thick with frictional liquid,
the clap of twerk & shout the same & gahtdamn, my ass
feels lovely. Feeling lovely, how much can a chorus jiggle,
refrain against itself before the slap starts to purple, hollow
into language rusting itself because, as you know, dear Reader,
it was hot when you got here & it didn't stop dripping?
It was chainsweating: a screaming sling, its wet-cry,
of metal & metal. This heavy bangled spell work, sweet
as the slump of my wrist. You already know how it hangs.
2am reminds you you can see yourself glisten. Smell us
from here: generations ready to be wrung out. The swelter.
The swagger. Extraordinary bass—it's stank. & I am alive.
In the air, a radio girl, swinging her glory sure as the Moon
sits low, calls herself a stallion. & who am I to think
I am any less powerful?

When My Family Says We Were the Regulars There

from that part of the country where our church was older
than the white folks owning the surrounding land & my mother
likely knew our enslavers, in our neck of the woods, one does
their best by not reminding them of it. It is regular here:
the name of their family the name of our family stretching the span
of this place's origins & everybody knows it. Trust. *Come as you are*
reads as *Bring us your best* reads as *You keep what's left*, meaning a slew
of field hands from the sticks that over time grew haughty: a history
—yes, we are tilling people, barely five miles removed from where
we met the Earth & picked the lint from its scalp, scarred fingers
scraping together single nickels making sure we were presentable.
Pride, our work & work, our refuge, we stitched that shit in our greet
-ings, caught it in our good sense, that is yes, we the regulars here,
the cooks, the cleaning, the choir holding even when the choir
can't choir no more—we be them niggas—at the door, in the pew,
in the hall, by the grave, in the night, in the text, in the week,
in the Word that was preached by the pastor in the morning
in the pulpit to the people 'cause of envy, 'cause we angry,
on the Sunday when we left there, it was December. We took
our coats & left them coins & wondered why we gave a damn.

Automation: Flight or Exit Interview with Holy Woman

If you trying to escape so bad, why you keep moving the same way?

In an example of animal life defying the assumed "usualness" of sex
-ual dimorphism, in bee colonies, where all males hatched are for the sole purpose
of mating with her royal governess, the queen bee is chosen & fed
queen jelly for expansion, procreation &, for lack of better words, ruling over
her buzzing drones & workers.

If home be the body, can you ever leave if you keep changing where it decides to stay?

Possessing very little queen pheromone, a virgin queen bee, small to inter-
mediate in size comparably when measured against mated queens,
can usually be found along hive walls, avoided by workers & drones.

How long it's been since you last made stars with your smile?

In the event of regicide, upon the sudden passing of a queen bee,
royal offspring are quickly selected by surviving workers to replace her
as "emergency queens," smaller in size with less capacity to breed
than a normal queen nurturing a hive, all within 24 hours,
preceded by an agitated roar for someone to lead them.

You ever bopped your head to the music of how he holds your name in his mouth?

Because her royal stinger is neither barbed nor thorny, unlike her workers,
a queen bee is able to repeatedly sting without injury or death.

You know running ain't never fixed nothing, don't you?

An old queen bee is not likely to leave the prime swarm outside of the swarm
-ing season or before knowing a new virgin queen has hatched from a queen cell,
mated & taken her place at the head of the hive.

Automation: Fight

If you trying to escape so bad, why you keep moving the same way?

In an example of animal life defying the assumed "usualness" of sex
-ual dimorphism, in bee colonies, where all males hatched are for the sole purpose
of mating with her royal governess, the queen bee is chosen & fed
queen jelly for expansion, procreation &, for lack of better words, ruling over
her buzzing drones & workers.

If home be the body, can you ever leave if you keep changing where it decides to stay?

Possessing very little queen pheromone, a virgin queen bee, small to inter-
mediate in size comparably when measured against mated queens,
can usually be found along hive walls, avoided by workers & drones.

How long it's been since you last made stars with your smile?

In the event of regicide, upon the sudden passing of a queen bee,
royal offspring are quickly selected by surviving workers to replace her
as "emergency queens," smaller in size with less capacity to breed
than a normal queen nurturing a hive, all within 24 hours,
preceded by an agitated roar for someone to lead them.

You ever bopped your head to the music of how he holds your name in his mouth?

Because her royal stinger is neither barbed nor thorny, unlike her workers,
a queen bee is able to repeatedly sting without injury or death.

You know running ain't never fixed nothing, don't you?

An old queen bee is not likely to leave the prime swarm outside of the swarm
-ing season or before knowing a new virgin queen has hatched from a queen cell,
mated & taken her place at the head of the hive.

Lavender Linguistics

The Williams Brothers, "Cooling Water"
0.0 mi

They slung "faggot" at me like I ain't know what I was.
I know I am nobody's woman—this body of mine ain't
built for chronic discomfort, but O. Still, a truth: most men
are feminine—reactive & fussy. At least, those I encounter

so. In my youth, I reaped & raved in sticky nightclubs. I danced
into further understanding: I'd carried my body with too many
restrictions. Binaries & spectrums. Projection or assumption?
—I assumed the form I'd soiled was spotty. In a bath, I came

to know ablution, astration, projected myself beyond the cosmos
& pondered on conventions: Binaries & spectrums. Projection
or assumption. Inflammation. The nature of swelling. The face
of the man that could grow me. The orchard of nature above

my head & fruit of its descending maturity. At any given time,
the youngest thing on me is my body, a soft reminder of still
another truth—all things that harden soften, in turn—a cycle
of hesitancy liquifying courage—an orderly thing, not quite

repetition. Order, inherently, not quite repetition, but indeed feminine
—responsive & flexible. I stretched & called my body *man*
& waited for it to sound like one. For one, it shut down & pushed
out something mannish—a consolation of second-octave greetings.

To my chagrin, they met me daily, graveling courtesies & unsettled
bottoms that got me in this tub in the first place. Such was their order:
they babbled like clockwork: gentle as a bruise, the lot of them
projections, the whole of me assumptive of only one thing: I know
I am nobody's woman. I have to bathe that peace of flesh. I must.

Boomerang, or a Chorus of Onlooking Fireflies Captions the Previous Poem

They smelled humid & lightning followed.

They hooded clouds & lightning followed.

They rained fire & lightning followed.

____ rained _____ & lightning followed.

____ hooded _____ & lightning followed.

____ smelled _____ & lightning followed.

Catfish

0.0 mi

I knew imposter syndrome was for the lonely
when it made a cannibal of me. Eight times another
image, I have been different people before.
Most recently, starved for company. I wish
I'd known they'd kill me, Icarian hybrid of Job & Jonah,
caught in the bowels of things set on consuming
me. I've fed thousands of egos before. Served my body
hot off the skillet & expected to still have feeling
in it, still fucking hiss & agree when requested to be given
away. Forgive me if I don't have the taste for it, don't give
a damn about plating such orders of service.
Memory is too tender, don't sit right in my gaping mouth.
O formant, o changeling, o beautiful ambrosia, I couldn't swallow
this before. I thought I thought all my feelings through.

I used to say: choose me. I will make myself whatever you need
me to be tonight. Thought I could undo my being's buttons.
Won't you look at me? Marvel at how I skin myself & press
my luck as only a shifty nigga can? I can scrape
the bottom for you, gut my form without even choking.
But, lemme stop throwing these bones before they give
me away, begin to yell. O belly, o tucked tail, o vinegared
underside, when I cut off my feelers, it wasn't long before I split
myself open. In two near-halves, one stringent, one spoiled,
I met my reflection in the fryer. O batter, o hell grease, o mound
of white bread, we sang the paring song of mustard:
Lord, I am not meek. I won't inherit this dome. But, please.
I have been here. I adapted. This is my ninth life.
I thought this meant I was good.

Spell

I lost the fourth-grade spelling bee on the word *assign.*
As such, I circled in rebellion against notions of power
every day since. I was warned: no magic could stop
the ways in which little things would undo me. I scoffed
& felt the sound itch in my ears, scratch how 45s, caught
in the jukebox Ma retires to the den, spiral in their filth
before arresting the throat of a needle mid-groove. It dizzied
me. Stirred the bits of my making the way lint emerges
at the sunset of a dust bunny surrendering to be,
once again, a collective of forms. *They're not even big,*
I said of their size, the truths of plurality winding
over my head, shifting from dust to vulture-flies eyeing
the rot of my humility with gravediggers' patience.

Off the record, it spins like this: a slew of rivals, a sob,
a choke, a chop-down, a corkscrew of buzzard-laughter
unstoppering a flood of tears longing to spew hot against
my cheeks. I am humbled, idling against the slow twitch
of my dying pride, looking my maker in their blooded beak,
the flush of shame glinting red in each multi-eye. I blink.
Watch my kaleidoscoping spiral. I know, I know what this is
supposed to be, know the less-lettered revolutions
of tiny certainties in full. They belch. I cough, conjure
up the word *refuse*, slowly round it out like *death.*

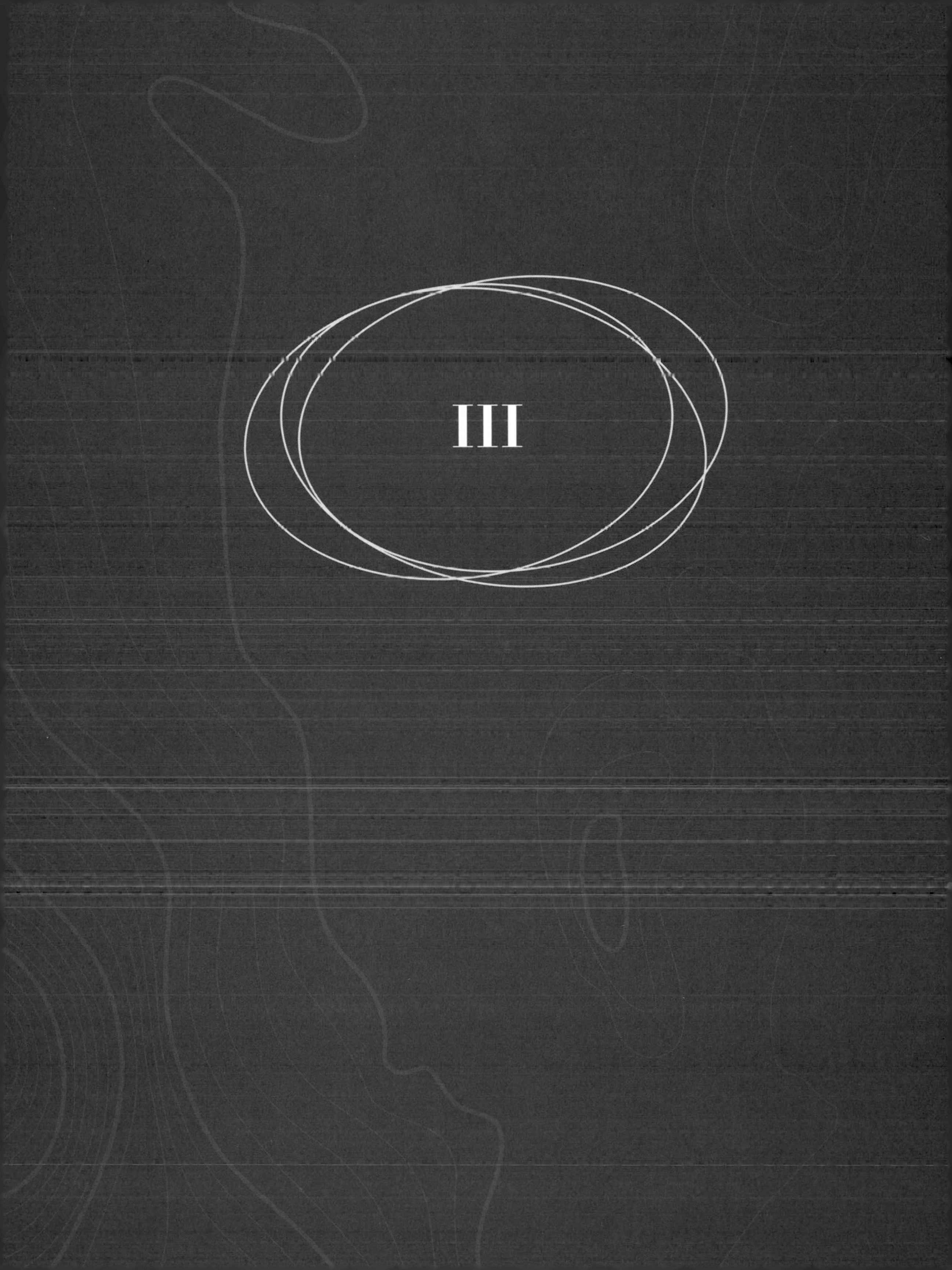

III

Boomerang, or a Chorus of Onlooking Fireflies Captions the Previous Poem

They smelled humid & lightning followed.

They hooded clouds & lightning followed.

They rained fire & lightning followed.

They bulleted mercy & lightning followed.

____ bulleted _____ & lightning followed.

____ rained _____ & lightning followed.

____ hooded _____ & lightning followed.

____ smelled _____ & lightning followed.

Hymn: So Many People That I Know

after Nicole Sealey

Beyoncé, "All Night"
0.0 mi

He is the Taurean kind of stubborn, that it takes
a lot to hinder, even more to keep—I thought
it would be shorter—this tryst, his urge to nibble

outside us & agitate my lonely, fevered aftertaste
only hours old, dripping out latent-like
—but alas. I have already paid for this concert.

This time, I am bargaining & he has yet left,
a nymph emerging by chorus, borrowed Anita lyrics
stuffing the muggy Georgia air. Tonight is a jar only God

can fit another love song into, a frail light
slung over the shoulders of my heart-hungry lover,
this move welcomed with off-key enthusiasm.

Sure, I have dreamed: lots of folks find love online.
But touch is not time, or permanence for that matter,
& we are not drunk & he, yet gone, & I pray this is longer,

this, in the cloak of song, one brief eternity, five
minutes all fears are lighters, swaying only for a while,
then snuffed out, as if all it took to rid us of them

was a bully of a thumb pressed to the lips,
insisting they not speak, only glow. It is kismet
—I know. I know he will leave all this one day.

Return Policy

Cesária

lips part / forks clink against borrowed
breakfastware, strawberries & waffle crumbs
scatter about them / hands part / orange juice
is offered in a glass / i wonder whether
my lover reflected in the bacon grease
still whispers to God while he pushes his glasses
up / hands clasp / i look at his fork / he pushes
strawberries into the corner / he promises to
send love when he gets there / i open my mouth,
truth shivers as if struck jam / glass is emptied,
his fogged glasses fall again / he drops his map /
i throw his glasses somewhere in the corner /
lips clasp / i squeeze my best bit of concern
out of a tube / we lie in the bacon grease /
we love until we taste the syrup in each other's
laugh, pray it give us one minute more to live
in the moment / lips part / we beg to make
dulcet tones like chuckles of last time / i try
hard to taste them / hands clasp / i strike
jam / lips part / strawberries fall from his eyes /
truth flies a foot over my head / he opens his mouth /
glass fills with truth shot across the room / hands
part / i clean up the crumbs / he steps on his
glasses / i throw away the forks / he takes
his plates / the corner smells like waffles / i wipe
orange juice from my brow / i try to remember
what love tastes like / he gets there / it doesn't
come back / i wish we hadn't stopped laughing

How Deep Is Your Love

1.
A robin gathers in heat
in search of a body of water,
   green acorns litter the sand
   & Memory says I am the yard,
   day-old puddles clustered at my waist.
The robin enters.
   Dips quick. Wet,

2.
a lark slaps
the whole of himself
   on me
& calls himself potter,
   throws a bowl of my body instead,
   the hole, shallow & wrinkled,
he, a boy in the country.
It is midday.

3.
It was morning.
   Memory says I am the sand,
   hard, hot, acorns a burn against the bird's belly
   just like the burn against his back; he is

4.
on me:
   a drawl,
               accented longing,
he, accidental thunder:
   a song,
               a clap down,

5.
a boy digging in a bowl;
a bird not in a ditch, but in water
   in a nook, spooned out by falling in;
a bird & a stone, two in hand
   in the hole.

6.
No, the memory corrupts.
   This is pleasure.
   I am the thrush,
   frantic & puffing to pluck
   more acorn caps before bathing,

7.
I am the bath, a breast,
   surely something tender:

8.
A bird.   A bush.
A sight.   A flash.
   Anything peeping struck—
   Memory: *Hush. Let him do his work.*

9.
I saw him.   He shook.
   Brazen stillness.
   Flight.

10.
The yard, still hot, still country,
his breath, warm,
   like rain,
no sign of feathers.

11.
Curious: if the bird came first,
would lightning have lasted elsewhere?

12.
I will ask the rain inside my mouth.
I know this water remembers, too.

13.
Memory: *It is an old tale.*
This, how it happened:
The boy leaves a maze.
The boy finds the birds.
The birds lift the boy.
The sky heats the birds.
The birds leave the boy.
The boy leaves the sky.
The sky tags the sea.
The sea becomes a maze.
The boy treads the sea.
The sea claims the boy.
A yard holds the sea.
The yard fights the heat.
The heat claims the yard.
The heat eats the birds.
The boy eats the sea.
The boy joins the birds.

14.
Still, an older tale:
this, how we happened:
a win on the morn, a bird losing wind,
a boy that I lost, a bird in the rain,
a rainwater boy, a boy I mourned,
a struck-down boy, a boy-winning rain.

15.
I put us back in the pastoral,
make us an oasis, our love a quenching well,
something large enough to bathe in,
large enough to whelm us.

16.
He is not used to depth.
He flutters over the shallow end,
chorals PJ Morton, asking me about size.

17.
He insists on entering.
I become the puddle.
He dives. I pull him out.

18.
I keep turning over.
He keeps turning up.

19.
I keep turning him over,
half expecting Crete to fall from his ears,
he, from the depths, Adonian & whole.

20.
He keeps turning up.
I keep turning him over.
I keep trying to revive a legend
or another waterlogged word I do not speak.

21.
He does not move.
He does not even sputter.

22.
Give me another word than *dead.*
I will not call my love that.

23.
He will not call my love that.
He will not call it anything.

24.
He will not call me anything.
He will not call me any.
He will not call me.
He will not call.

25.
I will not call him.
I will not call him love.
I will not call him anything.
I will not call him everything.
I will not call anything everything.
He will not call anything anything.
He will not call anything anything back.

26.
He will not call back.
There is nothing left to answer to.

27.
There is nothing left to sing about.
There is nothing to brag about.

28.
Give me another word.

Offering

we had seen the ghost roused before / quietly / one choir,
near hundredfold / humming / just one / forgotten,
at the altar / clouds parting after the last hymn / we had seen
a song bruised before / bled / like a stone / splintering
at every verse / blood showering / same choir, stoic / begging
to be near only one cross / i, thief-like / as if to make it more
convincing / we had seen a person gifted before / boxed up /
casket, offered / tinted blue / as if to make it more convincing /
no sanguine prelude / no tune on tap / only cracked reeds,
rustling / the sputtering of soil / slowly opening / to all
present without wine / ground hollering / here, you fools, here /
we had never seen so many lie at a funeral / but we had seen a god
petitioned before / persuaded / crawling, thick & balmy /
summoned / out of sixty or so mouths / hungry

Elegy

Cesária Évora, "Sodade"

they
never tell
                    us
how
to love
          a Black man
just
pat
                    our backs
when
                    we
weep for
          them

Frostbite

We are two trembling boys in front of my father
when I am confronted for slashing my brother's basketball
—I, the tallest, scowling of ruined play plans,

two strikes too far to turn toward apology,
not even belts can quell me into fear.
I shake in cold anger, the tip of my nose dripping
sweat in concentrated fury, the crisp chill of November's ghosts

groaning in tandem with my brother's icy cry-howl
—he disgusts me. Tagalong terror disrupting any chance
at moments of peace I have before sundown,

I meet my father's eyes; in the moment, omit all half-assed
attempts of him scolding me to deem him a bitch,
what *Ain't this 'bout* a precedes before blinking
back freezer-burnt frustration & one round of sniffles.

On cue, there are tears. There is silence. There is gall
—he shows up in my house years late & tells my mother
I have anger issues, he, a visitor to the tiny hearth

we heat by kerosene at night now, I, so far into myself,
warmth becomes the man that abandoned me instead of Willie.
They discuss me. I fail to locate a damn to give my brother
for not caring to hear another soft-hearted boy cry

in this house when it already creaks enough
—we are too cold for that—though cutting off feelings
is what the last man of the house left us to do.

He takes my toys, threatens something corporeal
as punishment though I am too old for that.
We are too cold for that, left with more blues
since Ma started singing country music on mornings

the stove warmed her more than her missing husband.
His note: sometimes we rid ourselves of frostbitten fingers
before the whole hand can't feel anymore,

he, missing everything he worked to keep warm at night,
too far gone to know he is my phantom pain,
jokingly asking just when I got to be so cold,
a wonder the absence lets him feel me at all.

When I Made a Puppet

after Justin Phillip Reed

Tonéx & Peculiar People, "Make Me Over"

I served my horrors in cold bodies,
got my 10s the old way—divas,
horses, orthopterans
—any legged sound walked.

That happened: I spun & split
a virgin cricket, lay it atop a bustling pyre.
Each ant famished ember—outside smoke
& burning core; I know necrosis when I see it.

Darkened, I prayed it under, six feet & severed,
called up old gawds to stop its writhing.
Silent, I thrashed both wing pairs as cherubs
newly christened.

I was fixated. I held grudges. I wanted to sink
as that cricket had, lace my legs
with rigor mortis, hobble
my wrists as drowning nymphs.

Each membrane flitted scales of mourning
—*Holy! Blessed! Dead!*—the struggle
of building a triad—Host, House & Surely
Haunted—without a stitch of dominance,

these, the versions insisting on slow tremor.
Each crack defied rest as ghosts
mocking their Maker, each an obol
denied a mouth on the boat to Glory.

Before becoming a Jordan ferry,
I bitched out boys that called me pretty,
slapped their banks 'til warm & frothing,
sopping Promise as rivers gushed.

Dank & young in missionary,
I held my truth the same as church
mothers—precise, erect,
steady on facing his coming. They came

rowing, riding, not getting off,
I found those days anticlimactic,
lost my scruples in lip service,
taking only what they took. They still

won't let me say acceptance; ask
how does one speak to such violence,
emerge from Yonder charred
as Orpheus? Listen. I have control issues.

I never thought twice about it:
how I pulled a bug to smolder,
legs to poems of their liking, propped
complete a chord in me.

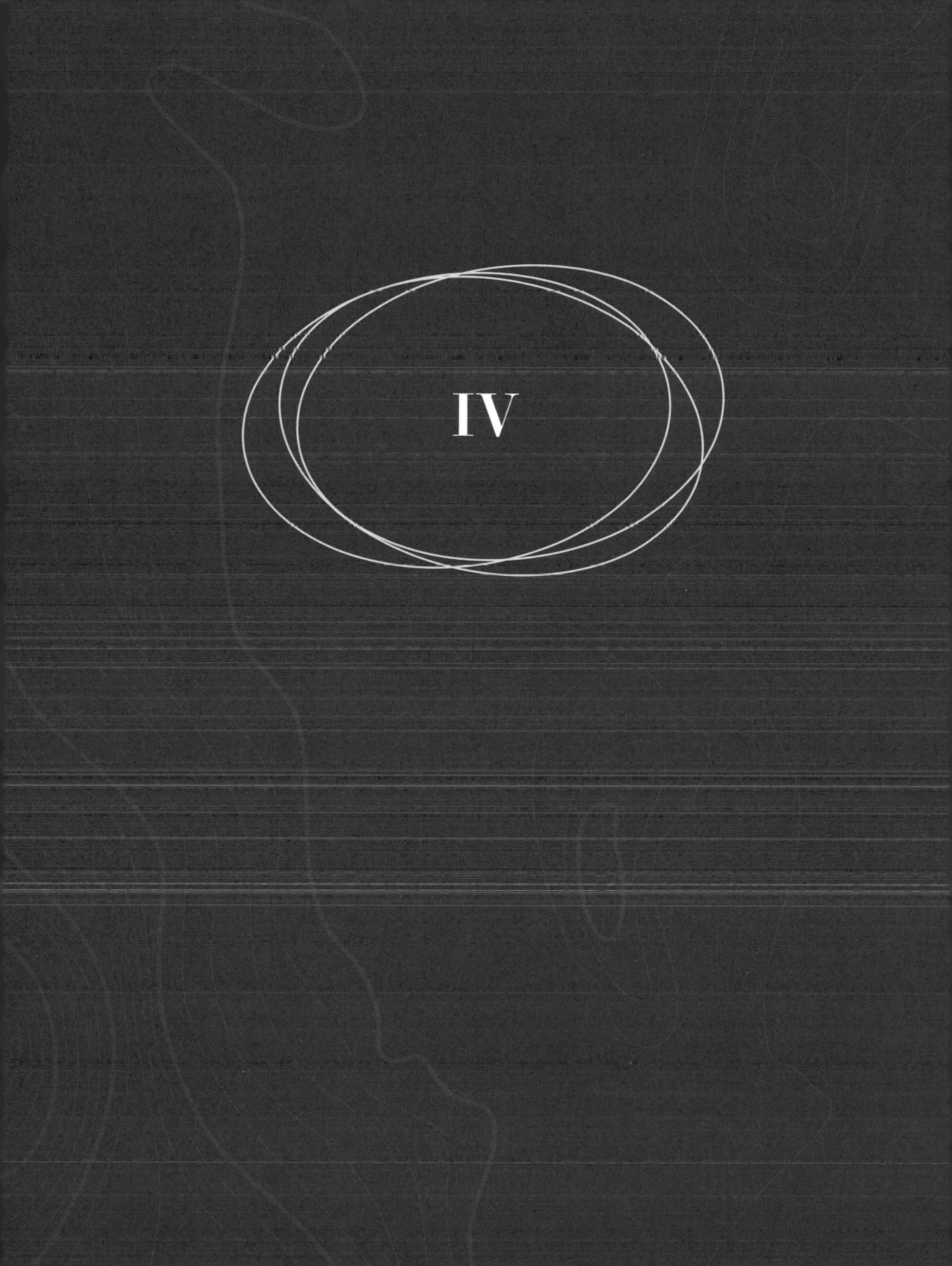

IV

Boomerang, or a Chorus of Onlooking Fireflies Captions the Previous Poem

They smelled humid & lightning followed.

They hooded clouds & lightning followed.

They rained fire & lightning followed.

They bulleted mercy & lightning followed.

Inverting, they wailed thunder; lightning followed.

Inverting, ____ wailed _____; lightning followed.

____ bulleted _____ & lightning followed.

____ rained _____ & lightning followed.

____ hooded _____ & lightning followed.

____ smelled _____ & lightning followed.

Something's Got(t)a Hold

14.7 mi

If I take it back, we are in the truck, on Bush River
Road, off some ditch of an interstate, some excerpt
of a highway somewhere in the country. Not far

from where Ma, my brother & I worship, stirred fright
& my father's best Sam Cooke descending upon
the day—grass, golden yet green yet, again, gold

—shivers as we roll to the bottom of the hill. It is September:
I, in the front seat, fingers exhausting the wheel of the gift
his girlfriend inherited in someone's unlikely passing,

let him borrow, let him call shotgun
for three-point turning today. I'm trying not to ruin it
turning too quickly, my brother wary in the mirror

I know should point towards the road. But, I want to look
back instead. It feels dangerous. I cannot quite explain it:
I always go left, wheeling over someone else's mortality

more than my own. I have not thought about death
like this for some time. Of my dark years, I never see
beyond the flesh of my casket, a pit of a dream,

my mother in black shades. I hear no sadness,
a projection I cannot let down, my brother clutched
at her waist, wondering why I am not here for us

to say I look as if I'm sleeping. I'm not sleeping
anymore, constantly conjure my passing, wonder how many
people love me, many miles I've gone. I stop around fifteen,

pause on a cheaper number. I don't want anyone
to pay for my funeral, bury anyone at the bottom of a hole
in a hill by the gold-green grass near the church I don't feel

I fully belong to, passing another dead end. I stop.
Consider other people in my decision. Remember the points
for making a full turnaround; go. In the other direction,

I keep my eyes on the road, fingers on the edge of something
sharp enough to turn into something tragic—I break:
remember the song playing, remember I don't want to hear

it in my father's voice without joy, remember my brother
asleep in the back seat. I don't want there to be a hole.
I don't want to be a wreck. *I'm sorry I don't want to*

anymore, I say. I'm afraid I'm holding something
I want to let go of. I'm afraid I haven't let it go yet.

Vocal Pedagogy

Love is a repetition of strokes demanding you wail on pitch during choir rehearsal & discipline is a lozenge swallowed one January evening until you hear the revving of your mother's 2001 Ford Taurus after finding the most gay-ass thing you could do after school. I, a pale fifteen something (*Pecan-tan*, Ma says), retire after seeing how many cough drops it takes to cry out *God!* for three hours, throat red all over. I am teaching myself to scream properly, a maladjustment to the following guidelines: 1.) Pain is a remedy; pain is a danger. 2.) Herbal before black, all herb before black. 3.) Black will keep you up all night, wreak havoc on the nerves. 3.) *Or the back.* 3.) Or the bladder. 4.) Arrive early to prepare it yourself. 5.) *Naturally....* 5.) Wet 5.) *or not at all.* 6.) Is pain.... 6.) *Natural?* 7.) If it's painful, surely, it must be working.... 7.) *Right?* 8.) *You expecting something?* 8.) *To happen without work?* 9.) No one cares if it hurts if you're not doing it right. 10.) No one's going to... 10.) *Let me.* 10.) *Teach you how to.* 10.) *Do it.* 10.) *Right?* 11.) *Right.* 12.) Again. 12.) Again. 12.) Again. 13.) *Again.* 13.) Again. 13.) *Again.* 13.) From the top. 13.) *Note, please.* 13.) *You.* 13.) Heard it? 13.) *Did you?* 13.) *...Are you?* 13.) *Even fucking?* 13.) *Listening?* 14.) *Take it.* 14.) *From the top.* 14.) Again. 14.) From the top. 14.) *Louder.* 14.) *Note.* 14.) *...Aren't you?* 14.) *...Are you?* 14.) *Aren't you?* 14.) *Well, I....* 14.) *Haven't...* 14.) *...You?* 14.) *Had enough?* 14.) My mother worries. 14.) Well, Ma, it is high school. I guess all the kids are doing it... 14.) all wrong, muscling their way to half-baked climaxes & running out of breath. 15.) Perhaps, I wasn't wrong in thinking this gospel could be gentler.

Automation: Fix

If you trying to escape so bad, why you keep moving the same way?

In an example of animal life defying the assumed "usualness" of sex
-ual dimorphism, in bee colonies, where all males batched are for the sole purpose
of mating with her royal governess, the queen bee is chosen & fed
queen jelly for expansion, procreation &, for lack of better words, ruling over
her buzzing drones & workers.

If home be the body, can you ever leave if you keep changing where it decides to stay?

Possessing very little queen pheromone, a virgin queen bee, small to inter-
mediate in size comparably when measured against mated queens,
can usually be found along hive walls, avoided by workers & drones.

How long it's been since you last made stars with your smile?

In the event of regicide, upon the sudden passing of a queen bee,
royal offspring are quickly selected by surviving workers to replace her
as "emergency queens," smaller in size with less capacity to breed
than a normal queen nurturing a hive, all within 24 hours,
preceded by an agitated roar for someone to lead them.

You ever bopped your head to the music of how he holds your name in his mouth?

Because her royal stinger is neither barbed nor thorny, unlike her workers,
a queen bee is able to repeatedly sting without injury or death.

You know running ain't never fixed nothing, don't you?

An old queen bee is not likely to leave the prime swarm outside of the swarm
-ing season or before knowing a new virgin queen has hatched from a queen cell,
mated & taken her place at the head of the hive.

Rhapsody, or Revelation, or Cerberus to the Fireflies

after Nicole Sealey, after Alysia Nicole Harris, after Lyrae Van Clief-Stefanon

It's a matter of fact: repetition dulls the senses.
Matterfact: I'll prove it, approximate how many exes
uttered the same thing upon leaving—*beautiful*
mind—kissing my forehead & dispelling into past tense.
In the void of presence, I thought there was more. Hope
—I prayed; there was more: chains, trunks of my own forest fires;
ashen scents, catching, in my throats, each musky regret,
rasping reminders that this was all there was. Yes, I begged,
I panted the way Black boys gasp in being choked
& finding God at the end of light.

In the beginning, I would not call me pious;
I would call me country, a backwood muhfugga enjoying
the shadow of their own howling. In the beginning,
I spoke & the dark rebelled. I sat & the dark rebelled,
threatened to extinguish the light from the singular
Brilliance I housed in the jar of my own body. I spoke
& broke open Brilliance—my pen pal, my own scattering
conscience in the void of presence—& barked to assume
multiplicity. Sure, my mind works as a hive, a clusterfuck
of blinking moments trying to isolate loneliness.

D'Angelo, "Send It On"
0.0 mi

Funny, isn't it—how even *compartmentalize* means
separation, means division, & yet, means structuring
against dissonance, to make a wheel of one's demons
so convincing they mimic Old Testament angels?
Yes, I'd be right to think I have no place amongst them,
but at a quarter inch away from ending the epilogue
that some will tell my children of, when it is all done
& there be no more cinders left burning in my throat
to call Love by its name or beckon for Joy in this song,
if You be watching:

1.

Baptize me by the barrel that held my moon
-shine, across from the bucket that I burned
my lovers in, buried my tongue in deep after kissing
their dust & sending them on their way to meet a man
that only promised them a one-room shack
on the East Side of Hell, but swore to them
that there was still room for good boys like us;

2.

put my pennies in my favorite niggas' pockets
& send 'em sailing 'cross the Jordan,
&, in the event they don't make it all the way there,
feast; shatter my boys, forward their fragments
to the Other Side, back into the grounds they kept
their paws on, their bellies bloated & striped as Christ
from, & my eyes darkened for, rolling up in praise;

3.

let my testament be the will to outlast my candles.
Pour me into the mold of a beast that dare be braver,
love harder than I ever did, stronger than the silences
between me & everything I could interrupt, dare live
fuller every moment flying inside my mason jars,
glowing without knowledge of an ending, but shining
anyway, swearing noisily without regret.

Aubade: Nocturne

0.0 mi

Harder, he pants into the scruff of my neck, our labored breath
condensing as my nigga pulls my hips into wolfish grind.
From a distance, we are two curs fogging a parked Chrysler,
though this, only half-accurate. In our nest, we transcend sex
-ed things, white-hot spangles like dead gods, the glow of us
pulsing brighter & brighter in turn. I have never shouted before,
but this is how he wets my nose—open, like a howl, a deafening
unhinging of worship—from the back—this, the way he whines—
throwing his head in praise. It is ancient composition, how we fever
the dark's bones, convince the night to do our bidding.
We collapse into each other. The moon of him eclipsing
the fullness of me, the rift of us unfolding unto new darkness
& what are we but ravenous? Here, we devour dusk, suckle
sides of cosmic gristle, mouths brimming, tearing the sky, Black.

Boomerang, or a Chorus of Onlooking Fireflies Captions the Previous Poem

They smelled humid & lightning followed.

They hooded clouds & lightning followed.

They rained fire & lightning followed.

They bulleted mercy & lightning followed.

Inverting, they wailed thunder; lightning followed.

In lieu of daybreak, lightning followed.

In lieu of _______, lightning followed.

Inverting, _____ wailed _______; lightning followed.

_____ bulleted _____ & lightning followed.

_____ rained _____ & lightning followed.

_____ hooded _____ & lightning followed.

_____ smelled _____ & lightning followed.

Automation: I

If you trying to escape so bad, why you keep moving the same way?

In an example of animal life defying the assumed "usualness" of sex
-ual dimorphism, in bee colonies, where all males hatched are for the sole purpose
of mating with her royal governess, the queen bee is chosen & fed
queen jelly for expansion, procreation &, for lack of better words, ruling over
her buzzing drones & workers.

If home be the body, can you ever leave if you keep changing where it decides to stay?

Possessing very little queen pheromone, a virgin queen bee, small to inter-
mediate in size comparably when measured against mated queens,
can usually be found along hive walls, avoided by workers & drones.

How long it's been since you last made stars with your smile?

In the event of regicide, upon the sudden passing of a queen bee,
royal offspring are quickly selected by surviving workers to replace her
as "emergency queens," smaller in size with less capacity to breed
than a normal queen nurturing a hive, all within 24 hours,
preceded by an agitated roar for someone to lead them.

You ever bopped your head to the music of how he holds your name in his mouth?

Because her royal stinger is neither barbed nor thorny, unlike her workers,
a queen bee is able to repeatedly sting without injury or death.

You know running ain't never fixed nothing, don't you?

An old queen bee is not likely to leave the prime swarm outside of the swarm
-ing season or before knowing a new virgin queen has hatched from a queen cell,
mated & taken her place at the head of the hive.

Ring Shout

after Phillip B. Williams

0.1 mi

some loved he's much how know to comes he hope i; life to back niggas

Work

for Ma

Ma taught me how to change a tire
the fall before it got real cold one October,
on the plot of dirt the pole beans we call Babel

spiral from, where our boozy station wagon
sat after hobbling home & passing out
in the backyard & in part,

where I've never not known women's work,
for the women I sprouted under learned to make do
without a nigga the same way clown fish change sex

when one is not present but become
just as lethal to make sure the oil gets changed,
which is to say I'm working with my hands again

as my mother's have had more calluses than mine,
&, sometimes, sound softer when the attendant
cops an attitude with her & we could use

a late fee extension, even when, some days,
she wishes I weren't as much like her—exhaustive
—in one pinch, doing the absolute most

—working 'til sore—arthritis, the remnant
left when we say things we don't mean
& our wrists get stiff from yelling

but blisters on me she still tries to tend to,
softly whispering, *Hold still; peroxide; witch hazel*
—feeble curses that someday I won't look for

the same men that she once cared to long for,
& Babel, the tower of beans we sang life into,
won't crack under the thunder of God because we

take pride in these few yards of soot we snatched
fruit from & learned to make dust a place
of peace in & I found my way back

to grounds I first wept songs over
& we wove one tongue, or grief,
or prayer, or scratching, or dialect from,

& we bless this space, our plot of dirt,
nursing home for Boozy the retired wagon,
so the two of us can stalk more beans soon,

for the losses that we have buried,
for the years I have been home, for our work
goes awry much less now, & for the inevitable

growing that we are sure to do here,
though signs say *restarting*; hiccupping
—signs growth lies in intention;

a willingness to adjust, make a stalk of oneself,
build; a scaffold of our origins—a jargon,
an argot bridge, a bent standard;

a way-preservation; an up-kept pillar;
a spire felled to keep our business
our business; our business, our pleasures

—most sacred of joys—the beans
we dirty our fingernails sewing,
water with sorrows while burying hatchets;

the hatchets, our shorthand—our cross
-hatch handiwork; our hackwork hacks—a hex,
surely something heavy—a limping wrist;

the wrists we wrap same as our tongues,
to know we can always apply pressure,
the praxis of pounding the point;

pressure, compounding when not let
up—where we'd like to leave our hands,
to let things be, because, to be honest,

we are grateful to have something
to be thankful for again, see green again
because we're used to seeing things spiral

but not always toward God; because we know God
to be in the center of what we do;
because we do what we must; because *We must*

get through this, we said with tight hugs; because
wrapping hardened things is how I learned to care;
because care is a field of love sewn asking

no return; because return is a cycle of love showing
back up; because showing up is a giant of a thing;
because, well, because many folks I know

don't believe in this sort of thing; because, to some,
ideals are as empty as idols & no one wants
anything modeling that sort of vacancy;

because my first role model was my mama
& loving people who can't do nothing
for you yet still is a kind of caring;

because caring begins in the language
but language don't always begin in care;
because language is ornery as upset snakes;

because upset snakes lie in the same places
we watered our joys, drowned our sorrows,
our sorrows mythic people disappointing us;

because disappointment is a parent, a side nigga,
a queer muhfugga that won't commit to anything
but the wrong damn principles—principles

in the mouth of absent people—an absence
of intention—an intention of staying with
an absence of intention—absent-mindedness;

mindful ignorance—a dedication to being
ain't shit; a bag of shit in the wagon trunk
needing to be taken out before we can reach

the spare tire; the reaches we made to patch
the only vehicle we had to get us through
rough times; those that tickle us

these days that start Ma's coughing fits,
because what is joy but stunning
plosives piercing the regularity

of breath, each an em dash refusing to yield;
the things we care for & make us happy
without context—a contextual Sunday?

—a day in the country; a country of modules;
a modulating garden; a garden of riffs;
a riff on an already embellished testimonial;

a praise break—a story—a multi-meaning;
a coda; a covenant; a promise to honor,
to keep our way; the choice to change *work*.
To *rest*.

Icarus Confesses

B. Slade, "Vagabond 2"

1.

Fine. I'll say it: a boy crafts himself of fable
& all the bards wind up faithless.
Ruthlessly pried open their throats
for sparrows & flounced my sweet ass out.
Truth: they won't claim what they have done,
the let-out paid the building fund & the saints don't
even know what ablution is but since *Come as you are* started,
my name was the only thing scrubbed from the record.

2.

To tell it as they did: of course,
subscription was just the beginning;
underpen his wings & watch him fall into the sea.
Let him say *order* & all the fallout blow back
into the eye, each lid rippling into a lash bent
in prayer, the count last at fifty sisters,
pointed upward, their god a solvent, one growling pool.
Let him say *silence* & he becomes the thief,
here a bag of feathers, his face hued red in the light.

3.

What is song but ascended flesh?
What I know of my father, he built of dirt.
I will claim what I have done:
I left before the door was closed.
I built myself of drowning hymns.
I stole every one to fly.

Revival

after Patricia Smith

0.1 mi

the preacher rises / polyphony / modulation /
jitters / cricket tony gestures / the choir inhales /
grass whistles / guitar swells / clouds saunter in /
the choir soars / tambourine flails / spirit surges /
cattails shimmy / fireflies dance / the choir moans /
another key change / clouds roll on their heels /
grass warbles / clouds leap / lone firefly dancer
blazes the aisle / counterpoint / the choir wails /
tambourine loses a bell / spirit looks around /
decrescendo / guitar murmurs / cricket tony coos /
cattails whisper / grass rattles / firefly pants /
clouds part / tambourine shivers / spirit exhales /
stillness / cricket tony kicks / the choir watches /
white sheet descends / unison / ascension

Notes

The speaker of "Self-Portrait as the Cricket" can largely be "followed" throughout the course of the manuscript.

"The Choir, or Chatteracks" is an epyllion experiment. The Choir it establishes later appears in "When My Family Says We Were the Regulars There," "Offering" & "Revival" & is the same one alluded to in "Self-Portrait as the Cricket."

The "Boomerang, or a Chorus of Onlooking Fireflies Captions the Previous Poem" cumulative sestet is a ghazal-like exploration. Functioning essentially as an onlooking Greek Chorus, the voice of the collective speaker emerges & vanishes as "six-word story" sentences, each rewinding & erasing as if in the six-second Instagram Boomerang flash video format.

"What We Wayward Do" alludes to the shape of the Greek ichthys symbol, an evolution of the Chi-Rho Christogram, known as the "Jesus fish" in American vernacular. Formed from the synthesis of chi (χ) & rho (ρ), the first two letters in the Greek word "Christos," a name & title of Christ Jesus in Christianity, the poem is a figurative play on the phrase "What Would Jesus Do?"

"A Tangle of Gorgons" specifically references Stheno & Euryale, as well as Perseus, the two sisters & slayer of Medusa, respectively, to imagine her as the speaker's gorgon ancestor, though she herself is not directly referenced. Both the overall form & its lines beginning at "in the center / of a lap in the center of a man in the center of a table" is a callback to "at the mercy of a muscle / at the mercy of a mind / at the mercy of a trigger / at the mercy of a mind / at the mercy of the clutch" in Justin Phillip

Reed's "I Have Wasted My Life" from *The Malevolent Volume* (Coffee House Press, 2020).

Exploring the classic art style of Grecian black-figure pottery, a ceramic technique known as melanomorpha (loosely "(B)lack form or shaped" in the Greek), the "Hymn" poems portray their actors as Black(ened) silhouettes in attempts to render the anonymity & distance of queer dating app & hook-up culture. This suite furthers this attempt by sonically blurring its title to mimic the word "him." Similar gestures are carried in "Return Policy;" "How Deep Is Your Love;" "Rhapsody, or Revelation, or Cerberus to the Fireflies;" "Aubade: Nocturne;" & "Ring Shout."

"Catalog of My Obsessions or Things I Answer to" is cognizant of its own list contents & thus, has alphabetized them.

"To Be Feral" & "The Vision" are reimaginings of the seventh chapter of the Book of Daniel, synthesizing the speaker as one of four beasts appearing in the vision described in Daniel 7:3–14.

"Labyrinth" references a personal phenomenon of the early 2000s in which nearly 30 individuals with my surname & a variant of my first name lived in my home county, simultaneously, resulting in frequent incorrect mail deliveries. The poem primarily occupies the allusion of the Labyrinth, a maze-like prison that housed the Minotaur, a man-bull hybrid of Greek antiquity, slain by the hero Theseus. Designed by the architect Daedalus, father of Icarus, for King Minos of Crete, the final couplet of the poem alludes to the name by which the Minotaur was known in Crete, Asterion. Derived from the Greek word for "starry," Asterion is also the name of one of the sons of the Titan gods Oceanus & Tethys.

There are 1,073,741,824 possible readings of "B{u/i}tter Pecan Apocrypha," depending on the reader's choice of pronoun, if one considers those in the title as an option.

The title of "The Vision," occasioned by the Mariah Carey song "Fly Like a Bird," from her 2005 album, *The Emancipation of Mimi*, alludes to the Icarian myth & another song, "Vision of Love," also written by Carey on her eponymous debut, released in 1990.

"Bush River Blues" is a list poem referencing Bush River, a stream & tributary of the Saluda River, a principal tributary of the Congaree River that flows through the Piedmont region of South Carolina & southeastwardly into my hometown.

The "answering" contents of "Automation: Flight or Exit Interview with Holy Woman" are automatic note-taking excerpts created while listening to my laptop repeatedly dictate a March 2014 Randy

Oliver article, "Queens for Pennies," originally published in *The American Bee Journal.*

The "Automation" suite—"Automation: Fight;" "Automation: Fix;" & "Automation: I" are erasures of "Automation: Flight or Exit Interview with Holy Woman."

"Lavender Linguistics" takes its title from a sect of linguistics that studies everyday language practices, speech patterns, pronunciations & lexicons used by members of LGBTQ communities.

"Catfish" meditates as one of the "cricket-fed & fried light" fish in "What We Wayward Do." Alluding to "Self Portrait as the Cricket," as well as the Marvel *X-Men* character Mystique, the poem is a play on the social media phenomenon of catfishing, in which one uses false or exaggerated photos on their internet profiles.

"Hymn: So Many People That I Know," borrowing its title from a lyric in the Beyoncé song "All Night" from her 2016 solo studio album *Lemonade*, was occasioned by the actors of Nicole Sealey's "virginia is for lovers" in *Ordinary Beast* (Ecco, 2017).

"Return Policy" & "Elegy" are loosely inspired by the lyrics of Cesária Évora's "Sodade," written by Cape Verdean composer Armando Zeferino Soares. Of Portuguese origin, "saudade" refers to a profound longing for an absent person or thing, "sodade" being the Cape Verdean variant. There is no word for this in English.

"How Deep Is Your Love," occasioned, in part, by the lyrics of the 1997 song "Rain" by SWV, written by Brian Alexander Morgan & Jaco Pastorius, meditates on a line in the 1977 Bee Gees' hit of the same name, covered in 2017 by singers PJ Morton & Yebba. It alludes to the myths (& deaths) of Icarus & Adonis in an attempt to explode or dissect a sonnet.

"Offering" meditates on the concept of "bringing in the (Holy) Spirit" while figuratively juxtaposing partially exaggerated ritual steps required to petition a deity.

"Something's Got(t)a Hold" takes its title from the James Cleveland gospel standard & considers the happenings of "Bush River Blues."

"When I Made a Puppet" is after "When I Made a Monster" by Justin Phillip Reed (*The Malevolent Volume*, 2020) & considers the lyrics of the song "Make Me Over" by Tonéx (& the Peculiar People), the former stage name of gospel singer-songwriter B. Slade before his leaving the genre for secular music.

“Rhapsody, or Revelation, or Cerberus to the Fireflies” is a typographic fugue, partially occasioned by Nicole Sealey’s “even the gods” (*Ordinary Beast*, 2017), “The Happy Couple,” a performance poem by Alysia Nicole Harris, & partially prompted by a 2020 master class by Lyrae Van Clief-Stefanon for the Center for African American Poetry and Poetics. It considers eternity, Sealey’s obverse form, & the nonlinear thought(s) one experiences during ecstasy, with its speaker(s) addressing the Cosmos & any divine (or assigned) voyeurs, first arranging their appeals as the stars of the constellation Virgo.

“Ring Shout,” an inversal of Phillip B. Williams’ “Inheritance: Spinning Noose Clears Its Throat” of *Thief in the Interior* (Alice James Books, 2016), takes its title from an ecstatic religious ritual of African American & West Indies origins of the same name, conducted in a counterclockwise direction.

“Work” samples language from Patricia Smith’s “Because” from *Shoulda Been Jimi Savannah* (Coffee House Press, 2012) & imagery from the English fairy tale, “Jack & the Beanstalk.” A lengthy meditation on the nature of work/life balance regarding the adage of “being twice as good to get half as much,” the poem itself is only two sentences long.

“Icarus Confesses” yokes the lyrics of B. Slade’s “Vagabond 2” & the happenings of “When I Made a Puppet” to consider an alternate ending to the Icarian myth.

“Revival,” written after Patricia Smith’s “Because” (*Shoulda Been Jimi Savannah*, 2012) & occasioned by the North American total solar eclipse of August 21, 2017, summons the actors of the poems “Self-Portrait as the Cricket;” “The Choir, or Chatteracks;” “What We Wayward Do;” “Offering;” “When I Made a Puppet;” “Rhapsody, or Revelation, or Cerberus to the Fireflies;” & “Ring Shout” to fulfill “The Vision.”

Acknowledgments

Sincerest thanks to the editors of the following journals, anthologies & publications in which these poems appear, sometimes in earlier versions.

The Adroit Journal: "Hymn: Chainsweat;" "Rhapsody, or Revelation, or Cerberus to the Fireflies;" "The Sugar;" & "Vocal Pedagogy"

Best New Poets 2022: 50 Poems from Emerging Writers: "A Tangle of Gorgons" (reprint), selected & edited by Paula Bohince

Boston Review: "The Choir, or Chatteracks" & "When My Family Says We Were the Regulars There"

The Columbia Granger's World of Poetry: "A Tangle of Gorgons" & "How Deep Is Your Love" (as "Bird in the Rain") (reprint)

Crab Fat Magazine: "Return Policy" (as "Postcard")

Foglifter: "B{u/i}tter Pecan Apocrypha"

Foundry: "The Vision" (as "Winged Victory of Samothrace")

Hayden's Ferry Review: "What We Wayward Do" & "When I Made a Puppet"

Magic: Poems (Everyman's Library Pocket Poet Series): "What We Wayward Do" (reprint), selected & edited by Kimiko Hahn & Harold Schechter

Obsidian: Literature & Arts in the African Diaspora: "Catfish," selected by Ronaldo V. Wilson

Oversound: "Spell"

Poem-a-Day: "Aubade: Nocturne," selected by Patricia Smith

POETRY: "A Tangle of Gorgons;" & "How Deep Is Your Love" (as "Bird in the Rain")

Poetry Daily: "What We Wayward Do" (reprint)

Pinwheel Journal: "Offering"

Shade Literary Arts: "Elegy" (as "Saudade")
Slush Pile Magazine: "Barbicide" & "Hymn: Throw Honey to the Wind & Watch Bees Come Back"
Voicemail Poems: "The Vision" (as "Winged Victory of Samothrace") (reprint)
wildness: "To Be Feral" & "Self-Portrait as the Cricket"

Additional thanks to the Center for African American Poetry & Poetics (CAAPP) and August Wilson House's joint digital performance series, *Feeling the Spirit in the Dark*, in which I was invited by August Wilson House Fall/Winter Fellow & CAAPP Artist-in-Residence Shikeith to perform earlier versions of the poems "What We Wayward Do" & "Aubade: Nocturne," & paired with the brilliant talent of dancer Jaylen Strong during Shikeith's Pittsburgh, Pennsylvania residency in January 2021.

I believe ascension first begins with accepting that one can indeed leave the ground. To God, I am endlessly grateful for the beautiful people who happened upon me floating & encouraged me to aim even higher. For the years undertaken in the creation of this work, neither it, its prunings, its many title drafts, nor I would be here without you:

To the incredible teachers & mentors who believed in my sprouting words & watered us as we grew: Dr. Florencia Cornet, Ms. Althea Counts, Mrs. Antoinette Kelley, Mr. Jeffrey Lampkin, Ms. Mary O'Dell, Mrs. Judy Whitehead, Dr. Kendra L. Ogletree-Cusaac, thank you. To the MFA in Writing Program at the University of Pittsburgh, for space, resources, options, & mostly, time: Angie Cruz, Dr. Shaun Meyers, Diana Khoi Nguyen, Lauren Russell, & my peers, thank you.

To the TRIO Opportunity Scholars Program at the University of South Carolina, CAAPP, the Pittsburgh Foundation, Poetry Foundation, *the Adroit Journal, Boston Review,* for opportunities & generous support, & the kind eye of Sister Sonia Sanchez in her selection of "The Choir, or Chatteracks" as the runner-up of the 2021 *Boston Review* Annual Poetry Contest, thank you.

To the artists, thinkers, writers & spiritfolk who fed me, challenged me, celebrated with me & held me accountable, my people, my heart, I thank: A$iahMae, Gia Anansi-Shakur, Yasmine Anderson, Honora Ankong, Lorraine Avila, Amanda Awanjo, Carmen Barefield, Jennifer Bartell Boykin, Niecy Blues, Brian Broome, Amena Brown, Kenny Carroll III, DeeSoul Carson, Kamon Cash, Théo Ceridwen, Franny Choi, Steven Cockerham, Coela Rex & Coela Rae, Concept Rxch, Quindell Conyers, S. Brook Corfman, Josh Corson, Kleaver Cruz, Ricky Davii, Ajanaé Dawkins, Langston Deary, Hannah Eko, Denise Ervin, orion flowers, Tanya Shirazi Galvez, Stephanie George, Braylen Gibbs, Jasmine

Gibson, K. Henderson, Shaquile Hester, Luther Hughes, Sabrina Hyman, Hakeem Iman, Fatima Jamal, Joseph Gunho Jang, Malvika Jolly, Candice Johnson, I.S. Jones, Vernon Jordan, III; Raven Joyner, Monica Kim, Sequoia Maner, Ashlee "Queen Keko" McCoy, Rodrick Minor, Tangela Mitchell, jonjon moore palacios, TyQuan Morton, Shy-Zahir Moses, Elizabeth Mundenyo, Nicholas Nichols, jeremy o'brian, Donald Paris, Jassmine Parks, Gabrielle Ralambo-Rajerison, Gabriel Ramirez, Julian Randall, Justin Phillip Reed, Catalina Rios-Hernandez, Brittany Rogers, Miona Short, Penda Smith, February Spikener, Edra Stephens, Francine Tamakloe, Daniella Toosie-Watson, Alfredo Trejo III, Steffan Triplett, Junious "Jay" Ward, Rev. Dr. Jonathan Wesley, Hassan Williams, Maya Williams, Phillip B. Williams, Mia S. Willis, & Patrick Wilson.

To Candace G. Wiley, Monifa Lemons & only the best Tribe at The Watering Hole Writing Retreat, for genuine love, fellowship & support, & to Jericho Brown & the 2019 Manuscript Coaching Fellowship cohort, for generous amounts of sage advice, exacting prophecy, time, rigor, & iron to sharpen against, for seeing me: I see y'all. Thank you.

To my N1HDA playcousins, for insight & true community, for the histories, wisdom, faith, & all the lit candles, sweet almond branches, jalap in bloom, & love, love always: Kayla, Zandra, Allie, Kendra, Tyanna, thank y'all so, so much.

To my siblings in song, Kea, Sara, Adrian, for the light & harmonies: I string this, in part, with the blend we loved, the traditions we kept & the Spirit we knew. May It ever stir us. Thank you.

To my gems, Francine, Candice, Asiah, Raven, for the love, understanding, & the sheer alchemy that's followed us since our first meeting: I don't know what I did to deserve the blessings of our friendship, Muses. Forever grateful to gleam in our constellation. I love y'all so much. Thank you.

To the baddest choir this side of the chitlin strut, for helping me believe in my voice, for the inspiration, for so many truly ecstatic moments, for the laughs, the love, for the music. My God, for the music: Trudy, Pia, Willie Mae, Barbara, John Earl, Nanny, Aunt Laine, Aunt Lois, Ma: I'll never forget that sound. I'd sing beside y'all any day. Thank you.

To Carey Salerno, Alyssa Neptune & all of the good folks at Alice James Books for selecting & believing in this book, for what still feels like a feverdream, an uncorked sea of endless thanks. To this book's wonderful designer, Tiani Kennedy, & cover artist, Liam Vries, better known as Vintagemozart, for sharing your talents & incredible, illuminating art, *Boys Don't Cry, They Just Hold It In*, I can imagine no better hands to have helped realize this work. Thank you so much.

To my siblings Nate & Sy & my niece Dani, for the love, continual airport support, & nothing but bona fide enthusiasm, my heart always. To my family, for believing in me, only love & gratitude.

To my daddy, for the time gone by, for what we both learned, I hope this helps.

For first hearing my spins at decomposition & reminding me language will wait on you to build yourself back up. For the prayers, for the love & encouragement, Mama: I get it now. I thank you.
I love you. I think I'll run on. See what the end's gonna be.

To my grandmother, Mrs. Bessie Louise Kinard, & my aunt, Jacqueline Robinson, I celebrate this with you. I know we'll have our time again. I love you. I miss you. Rest high. Rest long. Rest well.

& to you, Reader, for the magic of your curiosity, thank you. May it lift you; may it serve.

Recent Titles from Alice James Books

The Dead Peasant's Handbook, Brian Turner
The Goodbye World Poem, Brian Turner
The Wild Delight of Wild Things, Brian Turner
I Am the Most Dangerous Thing, Candace Williams
Burning Like Her Own Planet, Vandana Khanna
Standing in the Forest of Being Alive, Katie Farris
Feast, Ina Cariño
Decade of the Brain: Poems, Janine Joseph
American Treasure, Jill McDonough
We Borrowed Gentleness, J. Estanislao Lopez
Brother Sleep, Aldo Amparán
Sugar Work, Katie Marya
Museum of Objects Burned by the Souls in Purgatory, Jeffrey Thomson
Constellation Route, Matthew Olzmann
How to Not Be Afraid of Everything, Jane Wong
Brocken Spectre, Jacques J. Rancourt
No Ruined Stone, Shara McCallum
The Vault, Andrés Cerpa
White Campion, Donald Revell
Last Days, Tamiko Beyer
If This Is the Age We End Discovery, Rosebud Ben-Oni
Pretty Tripwire, Alessandra Lynch
Inheritance, Taylor Johnson
The Voice of Sheila Chandra, Kazim Ali
Arrow, Sumita Chakraborty
Country, Living, Ira Sadoff
Hot with the Bad Things, Lucia LoTempio
Witch, Philip Matthews
Neck of the Woods, Amy Woolard
Little Envelope of Earth Conditions, Cori A. Winrock
Aviva-No, Shimon Adaf, Translated by Yael Segalovitz
Half/Life: New & Selected Poems, Jeffrey Thomson
Odes to Lithium, Shira Erlichman
Here All Night, Jill McDonough

Alice James Books is committed to publishing books that matter. The press was founded in 1973 in Boston, Massachusetts to give women access to publishing. As a cooperative, authors performed the day-to-day undertakings of the press. The press continues to expand and grow from its formative roots, guided by its founding values of access, excellence, inclusivity, and collaboration in publishing. Its mission is to publish books that matter and preserve a place of belonging for poets who inspire us. AJB seeks to broaden our collective interpretation of what constitutes the American poetic voice and is dedicated to helping its artists achieve purposeful engagement with broad audiences and communities nationwide. The press was named for Alice James, sister to William and Henry, whose extraordinary gift for writing went unrecognized during her lifetime.

Designed by Tiani Kennedy

Printed by Sheridan Saline